At Dawn

by Natalie Lambert
illustrated by Kristin Goeters

Core Decodable 102

McGraw Hill Education

Bothell, WA • Chicago, IL • Columbus, OH • New York, NY

MHEonline.com

Send all inquiries to:
McGraw-Hill Education
8787 Orion Place
Columbus, OH 43240

ISBN: 978-0-02-133525-1
MHID: 0-02-133525-7

Printed in Canada.

9 10 11 12 KOD 24

I bought a book about birds. I looked for birds shown in my book. I could not find one bird. It was the bunting.

Dawn is a good time to spot birds. My dad taught me that dawn is when birds wake up.

I enjoyed visiting the woods every day before dawn. I brought my bird book. I looked for a bunting.

I hid in the woods. I crawled in tall grass. I fought annoying bugs! But I didn't spot a bunting.

In the fall, the buntings had to fly away. I had to spot a bunting before then!

It was the last day of August. I hid in deep grass. I thought birds could not see me.

I spotted a hawk.

The hawk flew in a low circle. Was it because of me? No, it was looking for food.

Small birds made loud noises. They saw the hawk. They tried to avoid being caught.

I saw a yellow finch and a blackbird. But I did not see a bunting.

Soon it was time to go. I had not spotted a bunting. I was disappointed!

I paused and looked at the hood of my auto.

There sat a bright blue bunting! I was overjoyed! I saw it at last!

I rejoiced as I drove home. But at home, I saw a second bunting on my lawn!

Then I saw a third bunting on my awning. I was ready for fall.